Wearing His Presence With Style

Patricia Anne Rooney

Written Word Publishing LLC
14189 E Dickinson Drive, Unit F
Aurora, Colorado 80014
www.writtenwordspublishing.com

Published by Written Word Publishing LLC June 2, 2023

ISBN: 979-8-9873088-8-2 (paperback)
ISBN: 979-8-9873088-9-9 (eBook)

Library of Congress Control Number: 2023909383

TABLE OF CONTENTS

DEDICATION

To my beloved husband of many years, Hank, who inspired me in this work and also to my family for their support during this time.

Soaring Higher in His Presence

Heavenly bliss is just a kiss away in God's scheme of things

A glorious plan, overflowing, abounding with promise

How could it not be allowed?

With the vows He has made and the covenant He keeps...for keeps!

The one who planned our birth to earth ensures our ascent to our heavenly home, escaping the scars of this world and its groans

Like a luscious pearl you wear around your neck and people stare

Wishing they could have one like it

It's my signature piece that brings lasting peace

Wearing His presence with style!

Let the lion roar!!

ACKNOWLEDGEMENTS

I would like to acknowledge Carol Jegou. Carol, you have given me strength and the ability to think big. You enabled me to answer this call and to count on God in writing this book. Carol, you are a savvy woman of God! Thank you, thank you.

I would like to acknowledge Peter Jegou as well. Thank you, Peter, for your special style of encouragement to me.

I would also like to acknowledge Edie Ward, my secret prayer warrior. Thank you for a caring heart, fully alive. Knowing I am cared for has been a blessing.

My Pen is Ready

My ever-ready pen is poised and positioned to write and record beautiful words—words of life, announcing words, and messages

Words of life

Words of direction

Positioning

Glorious words

Poems

Declarations from God to you

Glorious and holy and worthy

Amazing, true, everlasting, sure

Glorious, holy, true

Breathtakingly beautiful

Unforgettable

Memorable

Holy and true

Blessed, glorious and wonderful

REVIEW

I've known "Pam" Rooney, the author of *Wearing His Presence With Style*, for nearly fifty years; first as a godly woman who has had a significant influence on my spiritual walk. Next, for a sizable chunk of that half-century, she's been my mother-in-law. Being acquainted with her as I am—up-close-and-personal—I have to chuckle at the title of this book. The enjoyment of God's "presence" and the demonstration of one's personal "style", after all, have long ranked high on Pam's priority list.

Appropriately, then, her own style is prominently on display in this writing. From her genuinely unique and downright infectious enthusiasm for the things of God, to her use of colorful imagery, analogy and language, Pam presents a portrait of the rich life in Christ she has enjoyed for decades; and which she believes is available to anyone else willing to partake of it.

I use the word "enthusiasm" purposefully here. Its roots are from the Greek language: *"en theos"*; literally, "in God"—which nicely describes Pam Rooney's passion. She's a follower of Jesus who wants everything she says, does, thinks and feels to be anchored in her relationship with the fascinating Creator of the Universe. She longs to experience Him in all HIs fullness, and for every reader, every person to do the same.

Thus: *Wearing His Presence With Style*.

I'm minded of a saying by another author, Washington Irving, who claimed quite a while ago, "Indeed, there is an eloquence in true enthusiasm that is not to be doubted." That maxim certainly fits Pam Rooney.

Her luminous prose is irresistibly affecting. She identifies herself as a writer, artist and painter, called by her Heavenly Father to be an "outspoken vessel" communicating the thrilling realities of His Kingdom with her brush and her pen. Her goal in this book is to "paint a picture" with her words of His captivating ways and workings. Well, *that* she has done…You can say "Mission Accomplished"!

I heard Bible teacher Joy Dawson once pronounce God "the most exciting Being in the Universe". Pam wasn't there for that statement, but that theme is echoed throughout *Wearing His Presence With Style*. Not convinced? Read these pages…you'll see what I mean.

Sometimes Pam's observations act as a bracing fount of encouragement, sometimes as an exhortative poke in the shoulder. Once in a while, she delivers a loving, spiritual—and necessary—slap to the back of the head: *Buck up, Christian! Step up! Get with God's exhilarating, ever-expanding program!*

This is not a book about "religion" *per se*. It *is* a challenge to needy people to pursue a delightful, engrossing relationship with a gracious God who has summoned each of us to an endlessly engaging undertaking; often challenging, never boring. He's a God Who sent His Holy Son to rescue the world He'd created when it fell into dark troubles; and Who empowers us today to labor alongside Him. Pam's pleas and admonitions—whether presented in straight-on, declarative sentences or her charming, sometimes quirky poetry—crackle with admiration for all her Savior has done for her and anticipation about what He has for her down the road. And the book aches with a longing that YOU enter into familiarity with the same.

All that's left for every person who reads *Wearing His Presence With Style* is to ask the One the *Book of Hebrews* designates the "the author and finisher of our faith": "Okay, Lord, so what do You want for me?"

Written by Steve Pauwels

Steve Pauwels is son-in-law to Hank and Patricia "Pam" Rooney, husband to Maureen and father to Mike, Sam and Jacob. He pastors Church of the King of Londonderry/Derry, NH. He also serves as managing editor at Daily Surge (dailysurge.com).

Foreword

Written By Reverend Mahesh Chavda

It is with delight that I write this foreword to Patricia "Pam" Rooney's book, *Wearing His Presence With Style*. Pam and her wonderful husband Hank are longtime friends of my family and our ministry. I have had the privilege of pastoring the Rooneys for many years as Pam has diligently beautified and strengthened countless persons inside and outside of our congregation with an abundance of letters, cards, and gorgeous creations of art and poetry. I am thrilled that she has compiled some of her work in this manuscript to uplift and transform you, the reader.

Pam's own story of personal relationship with the God she has come to know so vividly will catch you up in arms of wonder and spiritual truth. He carries us through every season, in trial and triumph, love and loss, and then in love and triumph again. I have observed so often, during our worship services, Pam and Hank boldly stand up out of their seats in the Lord's presence and dance together, arm in arm, twirling joyfully in the rhythm of God's glorious Spirit. That freedom first came in a moment during a large conference when suddenly Pam touched Hank's arm and said, "We have to dance, now!" As they allowed themselves to be swept up in the beauty of His presence, the glory rushed in for all of us. A pastor told them afterwards that for forty years he had longed for someone to do what they had just done—dance together in worship. They have not stopped dancing since. The Lord has been waiting for us to take His loving hand as He leads us on a dance all our own. You, too, are a living vessel ready for filling, ready to take a step. Pam invites us each into His dance, NOW!

Wearing His Presence With Style is a feast of a fresh renaissance move of the Spirit coming on believers in Jesus. God pours Himself out in waves of encounter and miracles communicating the gospel of Christ to a world desperate for a good word. And we must learn and grow and begin to soar with Him. That is why this book is so timely and why it will touch you. Pam's voice rises in harmony with the psalmist, "My heart is overflowing with good news; I speak what I have composed to the king; my tongue is like the pen of an articulate scribe...Gird Your sword on Your thigh, O Mighty One, and ride!" And like the psalmist, Pam writes that in perilous times, "God's plan is from the war room." He pours out abundant life to overwhelm the designs of the destroyer. "There is no time like the present," Pam says, "to be lifted higher in God's company and His surroundings. We are people who go where needed and enjoy every moment and celebrate with God, enjoying where the action is!"

I won't give too much away here, but in the pages to come Pam shares how an experience with the artful golden script of monks of old, scribing beautiful words of scripture, set her heart aflame and sparked her passion to refine and share God's love through her pen and paint and see lives lifted as a result. With the lyric of her word gift, Pam imparts God's richness and extravagant love, Jeremiah 29:11, "For I know the thoughts that I think toward you, says the Lord, thoughts of peace and not of evil, to give you a future and a hope." Pam learned, like those artful monks, to share God's Word with beauty and with BLING! She reminds us that we are showered with God's gifts as with refined gold, and it is His pleasure that we receive and succeed in this life as ambassadors of His presence. We learn from Pam how the wonderful Holy Spirit of God coaches us, giving revelation and encouragement for those who need to know God and know His love. In the same way the three wise men worshipped the Christ Child bringing gifts of gold, He now makes us the recipients of His treasure until our cup runs over and we, in turn, pour that kindness on others all around us.

Wearing His Presence With Style will revive and beautify your faith. You are invited to taste a heavenly feast. Dive in with abandon into the sea of artful love contained within the pages of this wonderful book. You are a carrier of His love. Learn to dance in delight in God's love, ready for God to shine brighter than ever at the end. As Pam says, the "one who planned our birth to earth ensures our ascent to our heavenly home, escaping the scars of this world and its groans…How could we not jump and dance to this love song full of fire? Its' so easily done…Let go of the past and have a blast."

I am convinced that every believer can be transformed and awakened by reading and absorbing this amazing book.

Reverend Mahesh Chavda is the Founder/Senior Pastor of All Nations Church, Chavda Ministries International, and the Watch of the Lord.

Made for Your Glory... This is My Story

Plain as anything, right in front of me—like a well-kept
   secret—nothing hidden—opening up the glory

You are the glory maker enabling me to see deeper and
   deeper

You are the divine keeper of majestic culture and
   experience, not wanting it secret, but exposing the
   fullness

It is Your pleasure to open up rich passageways

My eyes seeing Your glorious touch

My hand holds the key

My life is not bland, but full of flavor and ever
   increasing easy access to Your sanctuary and divine
   company

Your sanctuary is ablaze with supernatural life and
   vitality

There I will cling myself to

Open up the glory to me more and more

You are the designer of Your glory

I agree with Your magnetic glory

I was made for the richness of Your glory

I sing praises for Your glory

I dream about Your glory

You have all the glory

All of my days, I want to be amazed and ablaze with
   Your glory

INTRODUCTION

We all have a story to tell. After I presented my idea for this book to a friend, God told me, "Patricia, this is a new era for you. Monumental and big, like you have never seen before. There is nothing to be afraid about, My dear. It is My great pleasure to give you the Kingdom, your gifts so clearly given and worked on. My delight is in you. I welcome all your wealth and plan for an excellent display of the experience you have been given by Me, for My glory. Way back in 2019, you had an awareness of My glory and now is the time to display My glory. Enjoy the wonder of your story and testimony and greatness that's in you. Exhibit the excellence and be glad. It's My gold—My value displayed in your experience, My precious one." His message was simply confirmation that this work is all a part of His plan. Reading the scriptures quoted throughout this book made me realize just how much God is involved in my life. It's my prayer that the readers will come to a similar realization and discover newness of life for themselves so they can be a beacon of life and hope.

Writing this book is my way of celebrating God's richness. I carry His presence in me and wear it with style—my own particular design and expectation indeed. I love being comfortable in His presence and using the gifts He has given me. Maybe this is a pattern we could all follow to experience God and His riches. In His presence is fullness and joy. Dream and celebrate with God. Everything He does is wonderful! There are so many facets to the Living God and the great love He has for His people. He uses marvelous ways to reach each one of us. All our lives are beaming with hope and expectancy. He highlights our life, telling us and reminding us over and over how much He loves us and His great hopes and dreams for us. He provides so much abundance which enables us to reach our destiny and find our purpose in life. It is written in Jeremiah 29:11, *"For I know the thoughts that I think toward you, says the Lord, thoughts of peace and not of evil, to give you a future and a hope."* All we need is a start and if we stay on the track and follow our path, we will be in tune with God's plan. Somehow, we are all masterpieces and when we follow His plan, He can stand and admire His workmanship.

Don't you just love the attention God gives us and how He watches over us? He answers our prayers, especially the Holy Spirit who is powerful and full of supernatural ways of informing people to discover everything they need. He is exceptional. He's the one Jesus brought to be with us here on earth when He was resurrected. The Holy Spirit is our advocate, lawyer, confidant, and problem solver. There is nothing as rich and more satisfying as when we, as believers, discover or become aware of a greater closeness in our bond with the

Holy Spirit. We must use this opportunity to learn and grow as we develop a closer relationship with Him.

As an artist, I was unaware how important this training would be for me. I had to yield to all the closeness and how much I needed it. When I was newly saved and baptized in the Holy Spirit, the Lord told me, "I want you to be a messenger to My people." I wrote it down and discovered little by little His unique way of communicating with me. After He showed me who I was and who He wanted me to be, my potential and my purpose became in sync. I entered the call without resistance.

I channeled into the gifts of the Spirit many years ago. Excited by what I am blessed to do, I often share what God has given me. The Scripture tells us, *"As each one has received a gift, minister it to one another, as good stewards of the manifold grace of God"* (1 Peter 4:10). This is what verbal and tangible gifts are all about. Enclose yourself with beauty and wonderous words to encourage and thrill your heart then share your art, creativity and giftings with others. That's exactly how God is with us and I've chosen to follow His example. I love being a messenger who has the ability to easily see an exceptional treasure of importance and the specialness in people that they do not see in themselves. I enjoy helping others find out what God has in store for them—to strengthen, unwrap, and be blessed as a Christian, especially. People need to be informed of the truth and their full potential. They should know about the way God created them and celebrate their lives and their purpose. I am so pleased and excited about God, that we have a relationship I can share and use to inspire people.

I have learned what affects me and what is important to me. I like to see favor, hopeful things, value, worth, and success. I enjoy hearing good results—a creative way of accomplishing. I love color, design and victorious stories. I am enthused to try new things and I love to share, especially to compliment and be involved with progress. I love inventing and showing achievement. I love to applaud and discover and encourage people with hopeful ideas. I love to identify the greatness I see in people. Recognizing their giftings is like giving them money or a big stamp that says, "Wonderful work. Bravo!" I love restoration so old things look fabulous, like brand new. I believe in giving away gifts and talents.

I am fascinated with words and art. My journaling allows me to communicate and give thanks to His Majesty, and at the same time I can open doors of thanksgiving and appreciation. I fill pages by writing what's on my heart. It could be something new and interesting and designs galore which await future art projects—presents, prizes, cards, notes. In my studio, I have surrounded my wall with little plaques. I give them away to help people enjoy and celebrate their name or a scripture because that's what ministered to me. Why not give it away to others? Art is to be shared. I find the Holy Spirit loves to suggest a piece of art to bless a friend with. My motto is "live to give." Never a dull moment. So, words and poems are handy using all my pens and paper to create awesome things.

Awe is an overwhelming feeling of reverence, admiration or fear produced by God who is extremely powerful, and awe is in store for us. It is a part of our inheritance. As plain as can be, God wants us to see and develop an eye for His Kingdom's possibilities—the full burst of His ways. They do not decay but are fully alive and vibrant and waiting for us to capture for ourselves. Enjoy and share our abundance with others. Let them come into our garden and see what's on display.

Let God's glory come into us in great measure. It will sever every part of us that is helpless, unknowing, and insecure. God's glory travels and takes up residence and brings refreshment to our soul. It builds us up and makes us comfortable, valuable, and more secure. It's the rain that pours and saturates us, cleansing us instead of hiding us. It will give us power and strength so we will not faint.

Put on God's glory. Let the light of His glory be seen. Be aglow with the Holy Spirit. It is important to think about and desire for yourself. Experience His love personally and enjoy His presence immensely. This is all part of the visitation and outpouring of His Holy Spirit at this time in history, most definitely! He shall burst forth real soon. Enjoy His visitation and be a part of it. It's overdue. Get ready. Be determined and expectant!

People should know their purpose and calling on their life and their destiny. It's so important when people discover who they are and who they're supposed to be. It helps them to live an abundant, fulfilling life. The harvest is ripe as we discover more and more as His believers. It is electrifying and real—a great abundance of everything we have need of. Amen to that!

Jesus said, "I have come that they may have life, and that they may have it more abundantly" (John 10:10). Why would the Living God give us scraps of bread instead of a feast? God is a very generous God and Father. He is the abundant one who stands alone as the one who gives life lavishly to His people. He wants us to have a larger measure of His greatness, love, and attention. Our lives are valuable to Him. I urge you to open your life to Him and receive His greatness and visitation at this time in history. This will infuse you and fill you with much joy.

It is my hope and prayer that readers will be touched and encouraged by the words painted in this book. I hope it produces a spark and a fire starts in their life and that they share the knowledge they have gained about God's Kingdom with others. May they be awoken and celebrate their life here on earth as it is in Heaven.

Invitation from Your Heavenly Father

Live under My presence, all of your days

O, child of God, rise up and let Me speak to you

You are not just an individual who is saved and no
more

May you enjoy My presence every day as My servant

I want you to join Me as My servant and leave your old
ways

Be rich in Me now

That is the key, your understanding of Me and My
Holy presence in you

I want to capture your heart, turn up the volume inside
of you, bringing increase

Welcome the more, the abundance I promise

I want you to jump in and become the healing guy/gal
and a demonstrator of My Glory that is in you and
wants to be seen

In you, I live and move and have My being

In you is a treasure, a wonder and one who
demonstrates, shows, reveals, and makes known by
appearing on the scene

Time and again you will succeed

In you is wonderous adventure

Be confident in your holy calling, not your weakness

I release you to enter into My glorious end-time move
of God the world has never seen

May My strength come upon you to override every
 work of the enemy
No more weakness
Only your magnificent strength be upon us during
 these trying times
Be glorified, King Jesus!

CHAPTER ONE

CARRY ALL THE GOLD

Gold is mentioned over 400 times in the Bible. A gold temple was built during King Solomon's reign. The Queen of Sheba traveled from Ethiopia to Jerusalem on camels bearing a large amount of gold for King Solomon. The three wise men presented Baby Jesus with gifts of gold upon His birth. According to Apostle John, the New Jerusalem which will descend from Heaven will have streets paved with pure gold. We are just as precious as gold and extremely valuable in God's eyes. We're all so different, unusual, and magnificent, crafted and molded by Our Father in Heaven.

Although gold is often associated with wealth, possessing gold is also compared to gaining knowledge, acquiring wisdom, and having faith. It also represents value, nobility, and was used in the Bible to worship God. Gold must be mined and then refined with fire, but the end result is purity and value. The refining process is often equated to trials humans must endure throughout their lifetime. Having faith during those times allows us to come forth as refined gold. And when we have faith in God, we are putting our trust in Him, thereby acknowledging that He is in our presence.

We are carriers of God's presence as believers in Jesus Christ. Be a carrier. Be a mentor. Be a messenger. Be a demonstrator. Wear His presence. God wants His people alive and focused on the new atmosphere He is creating. Grab hold of it. For the time will come and it is now that God's majesty and His glory will be operating at a much higher level and there will be an explosion of His love and guidance that will burst forth on planet earth. Expect it for yourself!

We must be mindful of the words we speak, how we speak to others, and when we speak. What we do and say encourages those we come in contact with more than we realize. Throughout the years, my husband and I have ministered to people we met on the streets and in stores who needed a lot of healing, mentally, physically, and spiritually. Doing so brings such joy. It's amazing how good it feels to pour kind words over others. The Scripture tells us, *"And above all things have fervent love for one another...be hospitable to one another without grumbling"* (1 Peter 4:8-9). Kindness, affection, compassion, and loyalty are acts of love.

There's no greater love than the unconditional love God has for His people. God is love and anyone who does not love does not know God (1 John 4:8). The Scripture tells us to clothe ourselves with love (Colossians 3:14). In other words, wear God's presence.

There are many facets to God's great love for His people. These marvelous ways can reach the multitudes who belong to Him. Each one of our lives are gleaming with hope and expectancy. The harvest is ripe for all of us. Let's gather the gold. Let us rejoice and be glad and celebrate His harvest season. Jesus came to give us life that we would have it abundantly (John 10:10). I want the abundant life that is a promise from Jesus. I need it desperately.

Hope deferred makes the heart sick shall no longer describe us. Our hope is in the Lord and He shall rule our life with His victorious hand. The King shall lead and guide us in His paths of righteousness and valor. We shall break through despair and discouragement. Our life and purpose belongs to God, the one who made us and designed us for His purposes. Rejoice in God, our Savior, our soon coming King. Lift our gates and let the King of Glory come in and transform us. Take back what is ours. Abundant life is what we shall apprehend. It was promised to us. It is our inheritance.

God's greater love and visitation at this time in our lives will infuse us and fill us with joy. Now is the time to open our hearts and minds to receive His greatness. Each of us needs to experience His greater love personally and enjoy His presence. Enjoy His visitation, enjoy His company, and embrace the Holy Spirit being poured into us. Don't just read about His love. Awake to His plans and expect to be filled with greater love from our Father. We, His people, are His beloved ones. He wants us to carry all the gold, and as we do, the Holy Spirit will continue to thrill us over and over again.

Incredible, That's Who He Is

God never ceases to amaze me

He does not ever make a mistake

He creates beauty and designs at His best

And He wants to have a glorious relationship with us

Wow, what could be better or more important than that?

I want to continue to discover, experience and celebrate everything God has given me and to share my bounty

Holy Spirit Coaches Us

Learning to step out in faith more

Growing and exercising faith instead of being stagnant

His communication enhances how we see God

The word "enhance" means to increase or improve

Heighten, intensify, magnify

Could we all use more enhancing?

The Holy Spirit communicates Jesus and paints a picture of Him

Scripture, understanding

How God expresses Himself through you will teach you about Jesus

Kindness and thoughtful things

You'll have experiences

Timing, plans

How precise God is!

The gifts of the Spirit operating in your life

God teaches you the lengths He will go to so you can communicate with people

His network is great!

No Empty Promises are the Promises of God

His promises, saturated with life and hope, hanging like
    flower baskets on the garden walls, along the street
    for all to see
Visible, tangible, bursting with life, "attention getters"
Beauty, design, no alkaline!
Alive with potential and rich possibilities, these words
    of grandeur
Time released fertilizer in God's Words, roots attached
    to their life source
Breathed with purpose, catching your eye, sign posts
    for us travelers to see
I am here to remind you, look up, can't you see?
Yes, touch them, use them to conquer and advance
Expect mighty things to happen
His Word is alive, come higher and aspire more

Chapter Two

Words Alive

It is written, *"In the beginning was the Word, and the Word was with God, and the Word was God…and the Word became flesh and dwelt among us…"* (John 1:1,14). We were created in God's image by His Word. He gave us the ability to speak, listen, think, and create. Once we get started, we can create till our heart's content. Words are powerful, rich in meaning and full of purpose. Words touch our emotions. They are a wealth of information and caring, allowing us to connect with other human beings. Words are free to receive the bounty and there's no end to the scribing of notes and sentences full of hope and treasure to give away. They can be used to encourage anyone and everyone. In my eyes, words are the fullness of my life's worth wrapped up in a package.

The more I write, expanding and touching lives, the more I am blessed and encouraged. We all need love, encouragement, values, and reminders that we were created for a very specific purpose and destiny in this life.

In my experience, I've discovered that you can design a book or write a note to bring delight to someone's hands and heart. I leave messages, notes, and signs around me to remind and enlighten me. I've saved greeting cards that I received and enjoy reading messages over again. This causes a celebration for me and brings an infusion into my heart of love and being loved. Look what the Lord can do.

We learn by receiving and are blessed by giving. We have been custom made to give, and the more we give away, the more the greatness of God's investment continues to flow into us. There is no end to the possibility of giving words of encouragement and strength to an individual who needs reassurance that they can make it. That's where my art and calligraphy come in. When God is telling me something, I not only write it in my journal, but I also make plaques and give them to people. One season, about a year or two ago, I made plaques with scripture all week then went to church and gave them to people. I just wanted them to have God's Word in front of them so they could be inspired in their walk with the Lord.

We can all use our creative abilities to design a card or plaque. We can mix colors to represent life, hopes and dreams. That's what painters do. There are so many options. Just experiment and see what happens. Write a kind note, add some decorative flavor to it, and give it away. It could quite possibly be rewarding.

Words bring life to me, especially personally. I am enamored with my dictionary and cannot live without it. In my letter art, I experience the design and powerful meaning of words. I went to see the Book of Kells in Dublin, Ireland one summer where lettering had been done by hand by the monks. They used inks from ancient ruins in old cities. That experience inspired me to scribe my own color style. I realized what a favor, privilege, and honor it is to be able to design beautiful words as I please. I can bring words of direction, hope, and meaning to life to touch people.

The Scripture is God's Word. It is written, *"All Scripture is given by inspiration of God, and is profitable for doctrine, for reproof, for correction, for instruction in righteousness, that the man of God may be complete, thoroughly equipped for every good work"* (2 Timothy 3:16-17). The Word of the Lord is there all along, waiting to be used as soothing vocabulary for all the ages. Excel with your giftings. This endeavor is at God's request. It is His pleasure and delight to bring His Word to those who surround us, to read, hear and enjoy. We are to be moved by the powerful authority and influence of His Word. He wants everyone to celebrate, rejoice and be glad. He is our wonder working Almighty God. His Word is just as alive for us today as it was in the days when it was written. Let's give thanks to our Heavenly Father for sharing His wealth and extending His Word to His people! Everyone receives the same benefit. And that's what He wanted all along. He is so outstanding.

The Lord is just a breath away from our innermost being. His voice and Word are valuable, pure and life giving. We should be pleased to share His voice with people of interest. It's the very slice of life people are yearning for. God's Word is beautiful in its worth and stature. There's a longing for His Word in His people's heart and soul that could never be sold or borrowed. The Scripture says, *"All the days of the afflicted are evil, But he who is of a merry heart has a continual feast"* (Proverbs 15:15 NKJV). God's Word is uniquely designed by a seasoned scribe in golden letters spoken by the King with glory and bling. His Word is the very ingredient we need for a merry heart.

It is written, *"for in Him we live and move and have our being…"* (Acts 17:28). What a divine connection that is. We are connected with the power of His Word about us. It is supernatural. His Word is not in vain. It invites us to embrace the power of His Word and His glory. People will wake up and wonder, how is it possible? He is at work both to will and to work for His good pleasure. God wants us to stay continually in His abilities. The Scripture says, *"For I know the thoughts that I think toward you, says the Lord, thoughts of peace and not of evil, to give you a future and a hope"* (Jeremiah 29:11). His pleasure is for us to succeed and be a part of His dream about us. We really benefit and have a relationship with Him. It works. Remember Jeremiah 33:3, *"Call to Me, and I will answer you, and show you great and mighty things, which you do not know."* God encourages us to call unto Him. So much of what God's Word says is just waiting to enlighten us. His Word is alive and active for our own being.

Now is the time to take God at His Word, receive it and act upon it and let it empower us. Let's celebrate when we find and enjoy God's Word. He wants His Word truly alive and working in our lives. He will train us properly as He opens doors for us. While we are living, moving and having our being, we have a divine connection with the power of God and His Word. The Scripture states, *"As for God, His way is perfect; The word of the Lord is proven;..."* (Psalm 18:30). God's Word is not in vain. It's not a foreign language. It is supernatural, alive and working, and full of life, encouragement and hope. Let's open the Word, dissect it, taste it, and see that it is good. Give testimonies to enlighten and encourage one another, building up the Body of Christ, and be confidently in tune with the Holy Spirit of God. When we hear His voice in our spirit, we should tune in immediately.

How could we bear to be without God's Spirit? We need His presence. His Word of life is our delight. It's a pleasure when God, our Creator, wishes to speak to us. Such intimate communication should be honored and we should be humble.

God is the very essence and it is He that we desire. He sets us on fire for all eternity. More Holy Spirit and less of us leads not to a lease, but to ownership in Kingdom Living. Alive forever more. All of your days, be amazed and ablaze.

In the beginning of the Spirit directing our life, my husband and I had a ministry with young people in junior high and high school. We hosted a supper one night and someone asked a young man to say the blessing. Listening to him, I thought, 'I could never do that.' The Lord spoke to me and said, "Open your mouth and I will fill it." He immediately gave me words to speak. It was an adventure and a breakthrough. I opened my mouth and spoke after the young man. My tongue just needed to be opened and working God's way. It was on the job training.

God trains us so well. He commits to saturate us and look what happens. Greatness comes. He has a skilled, unique way of communicating to us and showing us who we are and who He wants us to be here on earth and in the heavenly life. Our life, skill and purpose are not to be wandering around not knowing, but to be informed totally.

Sometimes, people are unaware and unknowing of the Holy Spirit. The Holy Spirit is more than willing to inform us and teaches us what our purpose is and why we were created. He cannot help Himself because Jesus has positioned Him as the advocate, trainer, teacher, and encourager for us, His people here on earth. He has answers and solutions. He's the key. He is what God refers to as a masterpiece. In the Bible, there are several reasons we, as believers, have been called a work of art and a masterpiece. *"For we are His workmanship, created in Christ Jesus for good works, which God prepared beforehand that we should walk in them"* (Ephesians 2:10). Could that be any more powerful or exciting?

The more we recognize our worth and value, the more valuable we become. It's essential to realize and seek out our importance and we can declare that this abundant life in Christ Jesus is for real. Jesus is supernatural. His flow of greatness is powerful and true. God's Word tells us to *"Rejoice and be exceedingly glad, for great is your reward in heaven,..."* (Matthew 5:12). We have one foot in heaven and one on earth. Let's celebrate and be glad.

Words of Delight

Words of delight
Like flying a kite
A most unusual flight
Up in the air with no care
Hold on tight with no fright
You will soar and enjoy the winds
Displaying strength to watch where it goes
Hold on tight
Hold it strong
You're in charge
Flopping in the breeze full of ease
Watch what happens
It's a moving fun piece in your hands

Early Morning Whispers from God

I awaken you every morning and herald the day

Your thoughts, My thoughts, they mingle together

There is peace in My presence for each new day, measured as precisely as every drop of a formula a chemist would use

You are signed out and My favor is given

We join hands and hearts to accomplish hours in a day

My joy is given beyond measure, so be at leisure in My company

I am able to do great things with pleasure

Be assured, My love never fails or runs out or is gone with the wind

It is complete and it covers, overturns, unearths all of life's situations

It is highly detailed and delivered to you at every turn

My love is unending and perfectly packaged for you, portioned as needed

You are on the drawing board and My eye sees you at every turn

With every dimension and possibility, I can sketch in the next part that needs to be in place for you at every one of life's moments

We are in eternity

Chapter Three

Be Encouraged

We are all unique and special in God's eyes. Without saying a word, we carry a message, a truth that tells the world that God is with us and within us. The presence of the Holy Spirit has such a distinctive and timeless approach to His love for us that He wants us to know. It's sort of like being married and having a spouse to talk to you with loving words. He wants us to know our value and the calling on our life. He's interested. He's curious. And He wants to give us more. People are walking around but they don't have their full potential running, like the motor is off. These words from God are meant to strengthen us and give us hope and spark a desire to want to know more.

There's a mighty flow from God directly to His people. He can put it together for each one of us one step at a time. He can amaze us. He will provide us with an intercessor to guide us along the way. The Lord said to me, "Let Me adjust all the many words I have spoken to you through the years. Get out the word you have written from the beginning when you discovered My wonder through My words to You. Be at peace." With this book, I humbly obey His command. It is my agenda. I gladly carry and give away, representing His Majesty, the King of Kings and Lord of All. I had a great time walking in His encouragement, fully enriched for years. I felt like a kid in a candy store giving candy away. God has such a unique skill communicating who and what we are called to be. We don't want to be wandering around not knowing. We want to be informed totally. I hereby present these words to all who read them as an avenue to come closer to God and a tool to be encouraged and move forward in their walk with God.

Love God eternally and follow Him. Walk with Him and talk with Him. Let's allow our hearts to yearn more and more for Him. Hear Him when He speaks through His mighty Word. His Word will find us, teach us and encourage us again and again. He will shower us with gifts and favor. Bring hope, favor and meaning to others by sharing His Word. Be grateful for your personal line of communication with the Holy Spirit. Conversate with and open up to Him the same as you would with a close friend. Prayer is a direct line of communication with Jesus. Set aside a time every day to pray. Jesus told us, *"Ask, and it will be given to you...For everyone who asks receives..."* (Matthew 7:7-8). Try it. Jesus is waiting to demonstrate His power.

While praying, don't just ask. Exercise your faith. For it is written, *"Now faith is the substance of things hoped for, the evidence of things not seen"* (Hebrews 11:1). Be sure to thank the Lord as if it's already received, faithfully knowing it's already done. The Scripture says, *"...without faith it is impossible to please Him, for he who comes to God must believe that He is, and that He is a rewarder of those who diligently seek Him"* (Hebrews 11:6).

What is in store has never been seen before and will get at our core. Don't stray and stay away from delighting in the Lord. Don't ever think we are not deserving of more of Jesus. No orphans in the Kingdom. The storehouse is full and we have inherited rights and responsibilities and assurance of our heir to the throne. Let God show us the throne room and our royalty.

Jesus also told us, *"...seek, and you will find...and he who seeks find..."* (Matthew 7:7-8). Look, find and see what God has so easily planned for our life. Discover our place here on earth. The enemy roams the earth looking to steal, kill and destroy. And although darkness covers the earth, as believers, we are to shine. Jesus Christ died and shed His blood so we would be united. It's a powerful decision, calling people all over the world to arise and shine. The Scripture states, *"Arise, shine; For your light has come! And the glory of the Lord is risen upon you. For behold, the darkness shall cover the earth, And deep darkness the people; But the Lord will arise over you, And His glory will be seen upon you. The Gentiles shall come to your light, And kings to the brightness of your rising"* (Isaiah 60:1-3). These are the days we are living in right now. Because I meditated on that scripture for a long time, I started to shine more than ever. I wrote it on small pieces of paper and gave it to women with hopes it would be embedded in their heart.

Jesus continued to say, *"...knock, and it will be opened to you...and to him who knocks it will be opened"* (Matthew 7:7-8). Don't waste time, energy, thoughts, or emotions simply dreaming about heart's desires. Knock and watch God open every necessary door, then take a leap of faith and walk through it. Let's do our part and watch God do His. The Word directs us to, *"Trust in the Lord with all your heart, And lean not to your own understanding; In all your ways acknowledge Him, And He shall direct your paths"* (Proverbs 3:5-6).

While asking, seeking and knocking, don't forget to continually praise God and give Him all the glory. *"For of Him and through Him and to Him are all things, to whom be glory forever. Amen"* (Romans 11:36). He gets the glory for our purpose. Rejoice in the Lord always. Hallelujah!

Meditation

The following scriptures are uplifting and powerful. Mediate on them daily. Reading them, I was amazed at the length God goes to for us.

> *"For we have heard of your faith in Christ Jesus [the leaning of your entire human personality on Him in absolute trust and confidence in His power, wisdom, and goodness] and of the love which you [have and show] for all the saints..."* (Colossians 1:4 AMPC).

> *"For I the Lord your God hold your right hand; I am the Lord, Who says to you, Fear not; I will help you!"* (Isaiah 41:13 AMPC); *"...I strengthen you and...help you'"* (GNT); *"...I, your God, have a firm grip on you and I'm not letting go...I'm right here to help you'"* (MSG).

"I know what I'm doing. I have it all planned out—plans to take care of you, not abandon you, plans to give you the future you hope for" (Jeremiah 29:11 MSG).

"...All you need to remember is that God will never let you down; he'll never let you be pushed past your limit; he'll always be there to help you come through it" (1 Corinthians 10:13 MSG).

"Roll your works upon the Lord [commit and trust them wholly to Him; He will cause your thoughts to become agreeable to His will, and] so shall your plans be established and succeed" (Proverbs 16:3 AMPC).

"Oh! Teach us to live well! Teach us to live wisely and well!...Surprise us with love at daybreak; then we'll skip and dance all the day long...Let your servants see what you're best at—the ways you rule and bless your children. And let the loveliness of our Lord, our God, rest on us, confirming the work that we do. Oh, yes. Affirm the work that we do!" (Psalm 90:12,14,16-17 MSG).

"Now may the God of peace...equip you in every good thing to do His will, working in us that which is pleasing in His sight, through Jesus Christ, to whom be the glory forever and ever. Amen" (Hebrews 13:20-21 NASB).

"For this reason we also, from the day we heard of it, have not ceased to pray and make [special] request for you, [asking] that you may be filled with the full (deep and clear) knowledge of His will in all spiritual wisdom [in comprehensive insight into the ways and purposes of God]

*and in understanding and discernment of spiritual
things—"* (Colossians 1:9 AMPC).

*"But I'll take the hand of those who don't know the way,
who can't see where they're going. I'll be a personal guide
to them, directing them through unknown country. I'll be
right there to show them what roads to take, make sure
they don't fall into the ditch. These are the things I'll be
doing for them—sticking with them, not leaving them for
a minute"'* (Isaiah 42:16 MSG).

*"One thing have I asked of the Lord, that will I seek,
inquire for, and [insistently] require: that I may dwell in
the house* of the Lord [in His presence] all the days of my
life, to behold and gaze upon the beauty [the sweet
attractiveness and the delightful loveliness] of the Lord and
to meditate, consider, and inquire in His temple"* (Psalm
27:4 AMPC). (*Note: A temple had not yet been
built when David wrote this psalm. He is saying
that he longs to be surrounded with God's
presence, enclosed and encircled with holiness.)

*"You have said, Seek My face [inquire for and require
My presence as your vital need]. My heart says to You,
Your face (Your presence), Lord, will I seek, inquire for,
and require [of necessity and on the authority of Your
Word]"* (Psalm 27:8 AMPC).

*"Teach me Your way, O Lord, and lead me in a plain
and even path because of my enemies [those who lie in wait
for me]"* (Psalm 27:11 AMPC).

"Wait* and hope for and expect the Lord; be brave and of good courage and let your heart be stout and enduring. Yes, wait for and hope for and expect the Lord" (Psalm 27:14 AMPC). (*Note: The Hebrew word most commonly translated as "wait" (wait upon the Lord) is qavah, which also means "to tie together by twisting" or "to entwine" or "to wrap tightly." This is a beautiful concept of waiting upon God, not as something passive, but entwining our hearts with Him and His purposes.)

"For God is working in you, giving you the desire and the power to do what pleases him" (Philippians 2:13 NLT).

"For God alone my soul waits in silence and quietly submits to Him, For my hope is from Him. He only is my rock and my salvation; My fortress and my defense, I will not be shaken or discouraged" (Psalm 62:5-6 AMP).

"I am guiding you in the way of wisdom, and I am leading you on the right path. Nothing will hold you back; you will not be overwhelmed" (Proverbs 4:11-12 NCV).

"I know the Lord is always with me. I will not be shaken, for he is right beside me" (Psalm 16:8 NLT).

"Beautiful! Beautiful! Beyond the sons of men! Elegant grace pours out through every word you speak. Truly God has anointed you, his favored one, for eternity!" (Psalm 45:2 TPT).

The God of Wonder and Majesty

I am the God of wonder and majesty

I am holy and full of glory

Act like Me when it comes to visitation

Be bold and speak direct words that will connect Me
with people

Don't be afraid to be bold and meaningful with the
words I will pronounce through you

Get ready to declare golden words over my people

I trust you and entrust you to bring My alive word in
these days

My people are ready and waiting to hear from Me

CHAPTER FOUR

VICTORIOUS DECLARATION

Turn away from the perilous times going on right now all around us and relax and be at peace. God is in our midst and He is in charge. He will clear a pathway of ease and expectancy that surrounds us so He can give us peace and hope for the future. He will give His people, those who carry His presence, rest and calm that will bring them hope.

Watch and wait for the thunder to roll in and appear. Listen to the sound. Surround yourself in God's glory. Be attentive to the move of God. History is waiting and God wants us poised and ready for what is coming. We will not be depleted or frail, but we will be strong and equipped for what He has ahead. God does not want us to miss the outpouring. It will be a monumental time in history.

There will be an overflow of victory. God outnumbers the evil one, have no doubt. Just call out the Name of Jesus and, as you do, God will show you the new He has for you. Call out His name right now, "Jesus, Jesus, Jesus." Jesus Christ is the hope of glory. Be strong in His mighty presence. Behold, it is He that is in your heart and He will prevail. We've got the victory!

Be patient, determined and expectant. God works overtime at His own pace and His timing is correct. He created all the time, it's what He does, have done and will continue to do. For all eternity, He will be at work. Open your arms and let Him cover you with His armor and strength. The Scripture tells us, *"Put on the whole armor of God, that you may be able to stand against the wiles of the devil. For we do not wrestle against flesh and blood, but against principalities, against powers, against the rulers of the darkness of this age, against spiritual hosts of wickedness in the heavenly places"* (Ephesians 6:11-12).

God's plan is from the war room. The people who oppose Him and operate with rage, revenge and hatred in their hearts will be up in arms as they do. His glory shall go forth and will confuse the elite. It is a perilous time engrossed with much turmoil and distress, but Jesus has overcome and brings victory and hope. He said, "The thief does not come except to steal, and to kill, and to destroy. I have come that they may have life, and that they may have it more abundantly" (John 10:10). Knowing that, we must not let ourselves be defeated. We can exercise our authority over this dominion and say to the enemy, "No more. I've had enough listening to your lies and deceit. I take authority over you, with your lies and hatred. I resist you. You must flee from me, now! I take up the sword of the Spirit, God's Word. Get out of my way. I am turning my back and taking Jesus' hand and walking in the truth from now on."

Self-pity may have ruined us, caused pain and anguish, and kept us angry and sad. But it shall no longer rule over us and cause us to look inward. How dare it attempt to afflict us any longer, causing us to blame others, seeing disappointment only with no hope. Command the deceiver to go, now! Our emotions have ruled over us long enough. It's time for our spirit man to rise up and be strong so the Holy Spirit can lead us.

It's imperative that we keep our eyes on God's Kingdom, His plan and our purpose. Stay focused and don't get caught up in the fray. It will delay what we need to be attentive to. If we get distracted, it will cause our spirit to be weak. Be busy and observant of our life in Christ Jesus, not circumstances surrounding us. That's what Jesus had to do. Turmoil was all around Him. His Father was showing Him, teaching and training Him to complete His purpose. So, it is with us as well. *"For God is working in you, giving you the desire and the power to do what pleases him"* (Philippians 2:13 NLT). Plead the blood of Jesus wherever you go. Change the atmosphere to love and victory. Bind the religious spirit and move above the fray.

The Lord has gifted us immensely, unusually and filled us with vigor for His purposes. He works with us so we can learn a lot from Him. He covers us with glitter. We will find wonderous things He has uncovered for us. He can't wait to open doors for us. However, we must agree to wholeheartedly, of course, keep giving Him all the glory, honor and praise. If we are attentive to Him, His Word and His Ways, we will be very pleased.

The Lord will use us to ease into His assignments—on the team of overflowing adventure. He will surround us with His glory as we flow with Him, bringing hope and enthusiasm wherever we go. It is part of our story. Let God put His touch on our inner flow. Our inner flow is unique and is the direct reflection of our relationship with Jesus Christ.

It is written, *"I can do all things through Christ who strengthens me"* (Philippians 4:13). This means there is more to come because, where God is concerned, there's no limit to what we can accomplish through Christ. All we have to do is please the Lord by wearing His presence and letting His light shine through us! This will make Him proud. He will be attentive to us as He watches us blossoming and showing His excellence.

The Lord will unfold newer ideas and designs we have never seen before. He will show us how things work and how we can accomplish new techniques along the way. Things we've never known or experienced will become common place for us. Receive it.

We will shine and advance quickly under God's leading. His Spirit will develop and progress us. Be obedient to Him and follow His path. His teaching will continue. Let's not compare ourselves to others. Instead, we must show ourselves as His distinctive eager students who can't wait to uncover a masterpiece. Be dedicated and full of God's hope.

We have plans and God has plans. His are superior and greater than we could imagine. God's plans are not locked up. They are all arranged in proper order for us to step into and fulfill. There are desires God has placed in us that we will sing about in our thought life, even now. So, don't be concerned about the technique or try doing it our own way. As we enjoy the adventure, we will show ourselves strong and willing. God will get the glory. Exciting and brave, we will have it all, even for eternity.

There's an awesome time ahead. Watch and see what is on the horizon. God is preparing us for new. Shout it out to the heavens. He has anointed His people for such a time as this. Approach people and speak directly to their heart so that they can receive and walk in it also. Be a link to God, from them directly through you. It's that simple! Remember, we are His messenger. Be God's ambassador of life and hope. Concentrate on the wonderful plan He has. Carry His presence everywhere always. Share His love, honor and victory!

Let the Whole Earth Sing His Song

What do you say?
It could happen this way, this very day and it could
 bring you dividends
Always look for the benefits
It is yours, not to store in a safe place, but for your gain
To explore, discover and uncover the best way
Don't keep it to yourself
Generously give it away
The Jesus App is filled with overflowing adventure
Why wait?
This very day, get to the gate
Why wait and wonder?
Hear the thunder and start singing His song
This is where you belong

Let Go of the Past

Let go of the past and have a blast!
Start new, it's for you!!
Revelation and knowledge are having the smarts
It's kingdom stuff
Downloaded from Heaven
The past warps and causes decay, so, it doesn't pay
Miss the mark and disembark and go backwards
You are off the road in a ditch with not so much as a
    pitchfork to help you
Sing a new song with me and we will agree
Freedom awaits you!

The New

The new is for you
It is not for the zoo
But it is hearing the coo of the dove
Reminding you that He is here with you
The new is for you
It can happen to you

CHAPTER FIVE

THE "NEW"

Miracles, signs and wonders—that is what we should be prepared for. We will see astounding things in front of our eyes. God is preparing us for the end-time phenomenon that will engulf the earth like Noah's flood. It was a problem for the world but not for Him. He had to sweep clean everything in the way. The cleansing occurred and people were swept away.

The "new" will be different. Occurrences of God's power will be so commonplace, it will open people's eyes to His ways, His strength and His love. People will be carried into His Kingdom. In Noah's time, they were swept away to death. But this time, they will be swept into God's life. When the outpouring comes, in His time, His way, newspapers all over the globe will know it is Him. "It must be God," they will say.

How strange and yet out in the open noticeable things will happen to bring a rise instead of pain. There is some internal order here. Where does it come from? God answered, "It is Me, moving around the people with a gentle breeze. Behold, it's Me! Never before seen like this. Move over, it's Me, Holy Spirit. I lead My people out of the darkness and coverings into My glorious glory. No doubt people will know it is Me. My signs will be everywhere, plain to see."

The refuge is here, the answer to prayer. We cannot continue as we are, evil ways defeated. All the nations will be aware. The Word declares, *"that at the name of Jesus every knee should bow, of those in heaven, and of those on earth, and of those under the earth, and that every tongue should confess that Jesus Christ is Lord, to the glory of God the Father"* (Philippians 2:10-11). It is all being prepared. The stage is being set for this end-time explosion to occur. The act is being arranged by God and the players are being made ready.

Evil men are preparing for destruction by nuclear means, while God is getting things ready for eternal results. His Kingdom is still at hand! And He will use His weapons in amazing, unreligious ways! There will begin to come to a halt many things that are completely crazy, directionless, and evil, and things will be brighter on the good side. Pray for the Lord to come down. Ask the Holy Spirit to surround and hover over us.

We need the presence of the strong and mighty One to cover us. We want to feel the heaviness and the warmth of Him—He who matters at this time! We have experienced Him coming before and yet this "new" is heavier than ever. What is happening, so strong and unheard of for sure.

Darkness is all around us. It covers the earth with a thick gloom over the people, but the Lord rises upon us and His glory appears over us. So, we shine amidst the darkness and confusion, bringing Kingdom reality and hope. Scripture tells us, *"Arise, shine; For your light has come! And the glory of the Lord is risen upon you. For behold, the darkness shall cover the earth, And deep darkness the people; But the Lord will arise over you, And His glory will be seen upon you. The Gentiles shall come to your light, And kings to the brightness of your rising"* (Isaiah 60:1-3). We are the light. The light could very well be something brand new that we are doing in our life, amazing even us. But rejoice that no matter what new we experience, this could very well be the "new" that we can beam about. New lights can be in store for us or someone we know. Change, advancement and shining galore could very well be on our path.

It is written, *"He heals the brokenhearted And binds up their wounds"* (Psalm 147:3). We can turn to God's Word when we are feeling forsaken, forgotten, and all alone. Although we may feel stuck, remember the Lord said He will guide us continually, satisfy our soul in drought, and strengthen our bones so we will be like a watered garden whose waters do not fail (Isaiah 58:11). How could that happen? First, it is a promise from God and He keeps all His promises. Second, He's doing a new thing in us and through us. Completely new things are necessary many times like starting over fresh with no mistakes and a clean slate to design from. Get used to these things. They will bring to us, give to us and help us.

Let the Lord adjust and rearrange new things in our life. No factors hidden; a perfectly free see-through life. That's God and it can be us. We in Him and He in us. The oneness is here to stay.

There is no one like God. He is the Best. His ideas and directions are golden. He created us in our mother's womb, remember? In fact, He knitted us together, all our inward parts in that secret place. We are fearfully and wonderfully made (Psalm 139:13-14). He wants to heal and revive our heart of compassion that may have been wounded. He comes alongside us to comfort us and whispers in our ears words we long to hear. He wants to affirm us. Man cannot do this amazing work. God created, designed and gifted us. He wants us to hear His words of life. Our confidence and ability come from Him, no one else. He doesn't want us to miss out on the purposes and plans He has for us.

We are who He says we are. Completely accepted, completely forgiven and beautiful in His presence. There is no other like each one of us. We are His prized possession and He loves us with everlasting love. Just cry out to Him, release the pain and all the rest will fall into place. He gives us great courage to do this. The Scripture says, *"...Be strong and of good courage, and do it; do not fear nor be dismayed, for the Lord God...will be with you. He will not leave you nor forsake you..."* (1 Chronicles 28:20).

God is doing a very new thing like never before. No longer will we be dismayed. This is a new day and things will be done in a new way. For it is written, *"Behold, the former things have come to pass, And new things I declare..."* (Isaiah 42:9). Suddenly, the "new" appears like a mist covering us like a garment. It belongs to us, God's people. Put it on to begin with. One size fit all. It's genuine, real to the touch. Let it be adjusted, not taut, but the perfect fit. Listen and learn with no earning. Live and discover and be not afraid. Everything is alive and real. A taste of Heaven.

Oh, how we will love the "new." It is created for us, God's beloved people! We will not just fall upon it. It's everyday air we breathe with no limit—no shortage of time in His glory. Splash in it and smear it all over. Get in it. Get wet. Drip, drip, drip with no regrets!

Know God's language and adhere, listen and obey. Agree with Him and let there be a flow in our relationship with Him that's free from clutter. Let's cleanse ourselves with the "new." Just as we are straightening and cleaning up, throwing away or giving, so is God involved with us in this area. Cleansing brings discovery. Space needs to be clear so the clutter cannot be seen. Once we have done away with the old, we will be pleased with the "new" in front of our eyes.

The Lord said, *"Behold, I will do a new thing, Now it shall spring forth; Shall you not know it?..."* (Isaiah 43:19). How will we recognize it? What does the "new" really look like? It's big and beautiful, like a neon billboard along the highway, supersized, dynamic, and real, and a huge deal when it comes alive in us. Who cares if people stare and compare? It's for God's purpose and for you and me personally. Plant the seeds with Him and watch beauty in the making. He will take us out of the realm of ordinary toward extraordinary. Viola! Let it be so, His heavenly showcase, orchestrating loveliness. It is His and ours to share. We make a beautiful pair. Engage with Him so we can see our unique beauty and His—intertwined and fully alive. We will never tire of His desire. Be aglow with His Spirit. He gives us hope in our hands and we can turn it into a piece of art. Think artistically with harmony as the Holy Spirit is at work in our midst. He will give us vision!

The "new" energizes us to sing and soar like a free bird. It satisfies our soul and creates in us an appetite for more. The old will cause us to waver, slow us down and create a crown of heaviness instead of freedom. God wants us to be free and on our own with no interruptions and burdens. He rescues us with the "new" for His possibilities. He throws a safety hoop around our neck. The E.M.T. is on His way!

Take a deep breath and welcome Him. Take hold of His mighty right arm. Let all sickness and disease be gone! Move into God's heavenly realm, His heavenly flow. His anointing will flow like a river and move into every crack or crevice where it is needed. Let's go forth into the highways and byways and announce freedom and deliverance to all we encounter. It pleases God's heart that we are willing and prepared by His Holy Spirit. It is written, *"Then Jesus, being filled with the Holy Spirit...was led by the Spirit into the wilderness...Then Jesus returned in the power of the Spirit..."* (Luke 4:1,14). Demonstrate His love and His power like never before.

May we be God's instruments, His chosen ones, going out on assignment with His Word, His heart, His touch, His presence. Enjoy and be surrounded by His presence. Laugh and have fun with Him, that is key. Let Him surround us and everything we do.

The "new" is deliberate and unthought of by man. God handles the far-reaching ideas and dreams that He plucked from the sky and fashioned for us. They are not only rare collections but specifically handmade, created with His emblems of royalty, stamped with His name. There's even an instruction sheet attached so everything works properly. Nothing is wasted. Everything is cherished, highly esteemed and productive. How wonderous are His plans for us—His people, His kin, His loved ones who are after Him. God loves the glory and He touches us with His splendor, so we will desire more and more.

We may have been blind to circumstances we found ourselves in, but one new thing turns us around and gives us a comfortable new chair—a new position, new vision, new assurance, and direction. It's all available to us.

The "new" will come upon us easily with no frustration or hard work. Embrace it. Turn the page and the "new" starts with us. Ease in with no effort. Only gentle breezes glide into the wind of God's Spirit. Go through the open doors as if they were curtains blowing in the wind. Uncover deep hidden things, oppressive things, things that control and hold in bondage. Break chains and yokes. Release refreshment, new hope and encouragement. Bring God's fragrance and glorify His matchless name.

Practice the "new" and it will work! No more jigsaw puzzles; only fine pieces of cut glass, masterful colors, designs covered with gold, declaring our newness. It'll be like the finest selection, an array of awesome at work for us. No secondhand pieces in our masterpieces. We will not scrimp on anything. Envision ourselves working with God in the master's studio. It is fully alive with scores of life-giving heavenly words. Reach out and catch what's needed.

Step up to a new level in God's presence. Go with His grace, His heavenly unction, His teaching, and His love today. Step into the realm of the miraculous like a magic carpet ride. Glide into it. God gave us this new thing and it will astound and delight our hearts.

Don't limit God. He has a depth we have not experienced before. It is new and refreshing and just what we need and want in our life. He will show and demonstrate His wonderful personal way, unique to the call upon our life. We will not be disappointed one bit. Great freedom and elegance for us. Drink in God's Spirit in a new way. This new season will burst forth fresh ideas and adventure for us, what we least expect. Reach for the stars. Make room and we will zoom and jump into it easily with much success. Heavenly hope all the way. Move with expectancy. The sky is the limit.

God has assignments for us. We will fulfill our purpose when we take on the task God has placed before us, the plans that He has for us. He has given us all some type of gift for a purpose and it's our duty to not only discover what that purpose is, but then to also fulfill that purpose for His Glory. Celebrate, rejoice and be glad. Know who we belong to, and with everything we have and do, bring honor and glory to His Name. Don't look back at the ruined city. Walk proudly to our next duty station. No lack here, only belief and hope in our eternal purposes.

For those who are called into this deep experience, it can be overwhelming. We learn and gain as we pursue more and more. Who knows what's in store for this wondrous pour. God blends and mends and overspends

His mighty work in us, causing us to display His wonder on many levels. He continually makes the "new" in us. Clean and methodical is His touch. The sky is clear and the water is soft. So, come sail with God. The route is secure. Feel the breeze, ever blowing to bring us hope. Sail with the Holy Spirit and desire for more as we adventure to walk in the "new."

Lord, have Your way with us!

For Such a Time as This

What better time to swing into action than now!

The whole earth is stirring, everybody's opinion seems to be peaking

It's in our face, with no grace with every news alert

Where do we go?

What do we think?

Where is this quirk going?

Does anybody have a map to follow?

Everything seems to be out of control

But there is an ancient way that does not stray causing us to feel helpless and discouraged

It is a mighty road—a well-traveled highway, a sure and brighter way to travel

Lift up your heads, O you gates…And the King of glory shall come in (Psalm 24:7)

The pathway moves beneath your feet

See the billboards along the way, like magnets, releasing calm and peace within reach

"To the Way," "Ta Dah" and "His Way!"

A supernatural adventure of possibilities

God sits on His throne

We are not alone

He is here with us in the glory zone

The Secret Place

Dwell within me, abide with me you say
A piece of Heaven on earth
A place carved out for me
A place to run to rest and be refreshed
A "go-to-place," any time, as long as needed
A reserved spot with my name written there
My niche molded and made for me
Help is waiting for me there
Encouragement cannot wait to speak to me
The walls vibrate with hope, surrounding me, embracing me
Releasing my burdens and cares
"Come in...be washed and cleansed...," my Lord says
No lies or accusations to listen to here
Only confidence and truth prevail in this place
Come drink of God's Spirit!
His sheep hear His voice most assuredly
You were made to hear Him speak
Listen to Him...can't you hear Him?
He loves you
He loves you
He loves you!!
He delights in speaking to you all the days of your life!
Psalm 91:1-16

CHAPTER SIX

THE SECRET PLACE

Our dwelling is our residence, home and the place of spirit and bodily rest. It is written, *"He who dwells in the secret place of the Most High Shall abide under the shadow of the Almighty"* (Psalm 91:1). When we reside in the secret place, we will abide, remain stable and fixed under the shadow of the Almighty whose power no foe can withstand. Abiding enables us to relax and focus on knowing we are being taken care of, protected, molded, and prepared. In the secret place, there is stability and security. Stay awhile.

It's a secure, safe, called to place. Not everyone knows about it. It's a deep abiding place to soak in and immerse ourselves. Not just a meeting place to have a chat. We can hold up and stay as long as we want regularly. When in want and need, it is a place of honor and refuge, where we are wrapped up in a warm blanket. In the presence of the Almighty God is fullness of joy. Get into His rhythm and flow. Stay fixed, positioned, poised, attentive, and ready.

There is no time like the present to be lifted higher in God's company and His surroundings. We are people who go where needed and enjoy every moment and celebrate with God, enjoying where the action is. High and lifted up in His presence. He causes us to excel more and above the normal. Be comfortable in the flow of the Holy Spirit and be confident in His great abilities. Keep our head held high and close to Him. These days are going to keep us on our toes as we witness His honor, dignity and power. His people will shine and be noticeable, like the early church, out in the open, demonstrating Him, not themselves. Get ready for upheaval. We will remain calm and important in His eyes for the work He wants us involved in. Our steadiness and strength are very noticeable like when we dance in His presence.

Scripture tells us to praise His name with the dance (Psalm 149:3). Dancing to glorious, anointed music and singing words to the Living God is an amazing tribute to our Beloved King. The first time I broke out in song and dance I heard the lyrics, "Dance with me O' lover of my soul to the song of all songs." Hearing and agreeing with that beautiful song caused me to react in the Spirit and display. How could we not jump and dance to this love song full of fire? It was simply outstanding to be a part of dancing in the glory. Dancing in His presence was so easily done. My husband and I waited to catch the perfect beat, knowing or hoping we would get the right signal to dance. There was a large conference going on. During worship, we were standing up and suddenly, I felt weak with a heavy metal cover on me. I touched my husband and said, "We have to dance now." As we danced, strength came into my body. Afterwards, a pastor in the audience told us he had been waiting for 40 years to see a couple dance in the presence like that.

When God wants us to do something, we have to move right away and rely on Him. He knows what's going to happen. Say, "yes" to the Holy Spirit. Embrace it as it cleanses, heals and gives us new strength. Trust and obey God, even if we don't know the purpose right away. Get ready for this great move of God's Spirit. His presence will be seen and heard like never before with gusto. Wild and furious will come and people will be swept up into His arms. Get ready. He will have His day!

Realize that our worth is important to God. It's essential to the times we're living in. See value in life and know we are God's precious people. The way He talks about us, provides guidance, and keeps promises scribed in the Bible, His beautiful written Word, makes it clear that He is for us. I am in awe of how much God wants to communicate with His people. We are His people, His flock. He sees into us and reveals Himself in a particular way with each person. He knows our destiny and exactly what we need so we can become the person we are meant to be. There is something very fulfilling in this for each one of us.

We have been birthed in the natural and experience. But now, as born again believers, with supernatural ways, we discover our true selves in our life. We grow in the natural in the womb (that special place) and then we have to learn our true identity God's way with His revelation and His presence within us. And as we progress and grow through and with Christ Jesus, we eventually reside in the secret place. How wonderful!

We are carriers of His divine presence wherever we travel to and whatever company we are in. We are in a place of honor, representing God's Kingdom, just as an ambassador represents his leadership in another country and is loyal to his president. We represent the Kingdom of God, adhering to leaders and God's Word along our path here on earth. The Spirit of God is truly alive within us.

I remember how I felt on a snowy day in New Haven, Connecticut. My husband and I met with some people who prayed with us to receive the Holy Spirit. It was exciting to encounter our beloved Holy Spirit of the Living God in us, to start a new journey together with new places, new groups of people and under God's watchful eye. It has been an adventure with much joy to learn and do then and now.

Prior to that wonderful experience, I had a miscarriage and lost a son. God ministered to me when I returned to my bed. He reminded me how He had to give up His Son. I saw His Hand giving Him up. God continued with these words, "You will not have a son, but you will have a great measure of the Son to give to many people." Giving to many people has indeed been my specialty all these years.

It's important to take hold of our specialty in the Kingdom of God and know what He has called us to be as we live and move. Aim to dwell in the secret place of the Most High. Desire to be a part of His glory bubble. He will show us His glory in a mighty way. It will touch us and grab our attention. Be amazed and full of God's glory and majesty all the days of our life. Let His glory be upon us in every situation. Let Him use us to bring His glory to others. His glory is heavenly and full of promise. Stand in agreement with His glory. We were made for His glory.

The Gift, The Promise

Dearest Lord, thank You for normalcy in our
    relationship
It is so wonderful to talk things out
I just want to say, thank You
Thank You, most wonderful, for what You have done
    for us in healing, restoring and making us whole for
    Your purposes
I am most grateful, dearest One
You are magnificent
Your greatness to be seen
Noticeable
Recognizable
Important
Substantial
Valuable
Understood
Viable
Fabulous
Spot On
Great and Mighty is the Lord our God
You are worthy of all praise and glory
You alone are worthy
Blessed be Your Holy Name, forever and ever

Heaven's Brochure: What's it Like?

You alone are worthy of all praise and honor, Your
   Majesty
Thousands of thunderous words cannot express the
   story of Your amazing ways
Who You are fills the universe with vibrant life
There is not a single spot Your presence does not touch
Vast passageways yet to be discovered and traveled
Winding paths and deep horizons await Your footsteps
Our eyes will one day feast on Heaven
O, the glory that awaits us
I've heard the color display is breathtaking and the
   flowers and blades of grass vibrate and sing
Did You not say in John 14:2, "In My Father's house
   are many mansions; if it were not so, I would have
   told you. I go to prepare a place for you"?
I place my trust in You
I walk with You daily

Have you read the brochure?
Reservations are required
Is your name written in the Lamb's Book of Life?
Just sign your name on the dotted line!

CHAPTER SEVEN

HEAVEN'S BROCHURE

If you're going on a trip, you want to have brochures about what you're going to see there. Have you read Heaven's brochure? The Bible does not tell us everything we desire to know about Heaven, but it does tell us enough to know that Heaven is God's dwelling place (Psalm 33:13; John 14:2) where Jesus Christ is today (Acts 1:11) where Christians go when they die (Philippians 1:21-23). It's a city in paradise (Luke 23:43), full of mansions (John 14:2), designed and built by God (Hebrews 11:10), where the streets are paved with gold, the gates are made of pearl, and the walls made of precious jewels (Revelation 21). It's a wonderful place.

I haven't seen any visions of Heaven or been taken to Heaven, but I know of people who have. They all say it's a magnificent place. When my mother was older, I would read to her. There were hardly any books written about Heaven. Anything I knew, I would tell her because I knew she was going to go to Heaven. We prayed and she received the Lord. I'm looking forward to seeing her again when I get there.

Philippians 3:20 says, *"For our citizenship is in heaven, from which we also eagerly wait for the Savior, the Lord Jesus Christ."* Reservations in the Book of Life are required to enter the gates of Heaven. The Scripture tells us, *"And the dead were judged according to their works, by the things which were written in the books...And anyone not found written in the Book of Life was cast into the lake of fire"* (Revelation 20:12,15). This means, if your name is not in the Book of Life, you cannot enter Heaven's gates. Well, how do you make that reservation? How does your name get written in the Book of Life? One thing we must do is follow God's commandments.

No one is perfect, but we can all do our best to live a sinless life. The Lord told Moses, "Whoever has sinned against Me, I will blot him out of My book" (Exodus 32:33). Follow God's commandments and live by His laws so your name will not be blotted out. The Lord pays attention to what we do here on earth. He takes notes of remembrance when we praise Him, worship Him and obey Him. He watches us as we wear His presence with style. Do all these things then *"...rejoice because your names are written in heaven"* (Luke 10:20).

Too many people have hearts of stone. We need to have our heart clean and make a marvelous move, not just for a season but for eternity. Ask the Lord for a brand new heart ready to serve and be with Him forever in Heaven. When we receive a new heart, it's heavenly. The key to Heaven. The Holy Spirit will guide us and teach us along the way.

While Heaven is seen as where we will live our eternal life, did you know that we can also experience Heaven here on earth? The Lord's Prayer in Luke 11:2 says, "Your kingdom come. Your will be done on earth as it is in Heaven." The Kingdom of God is within us (Luke 17:21). The Kingdom is when Heaven's attributes—righteousness, peace, and joy—invade the earth. When we understand how God does things, become who God said we are, and possess what God said we can have, we can experience Heaven here on earth.

In Daniel 7:22, it was prophesied that when Jesus came (the ancient of days), judgment was given for the saints of the Most High (God's people) and the time came when the saints possess the Kingdom. Jesus has come so it's been time for us to possess the Kingdom of God. All we have to do is seek what's important to Jesus first and live righteously, and all these things will be added to us (Matthew 6:33). What things? The "new," grace, favor, blessings, peace, joy, healing, deliverance, forgiveness, fulfillment of all God's promises, and anything and everything we can imagine or ask for. I am in awe of all that is available.

We have one foot in Heaven and one foot here on earth. We're going to go there but we need to take advantage of all these opportunities in our lifetime. It is written, *"And all these blessings shall come upon you and overtake you, because you obey the voice of the Lord your God"* (Deuteronomy 28:2). God is going to unlock all our gifts and talents. Use them to be a blessing to others and fulfill God's will here on earth as it is in Heaven. Hallelujah!

Glorious One

Open up the heavens
    Let Your love come down
    Mighty love, liquid love
    Flowing streams…glowing sunbeams
    Eternal fire to inspire and change us
Awakening love we long for
    Awakening fire to set us ablaze
    Living torches, igniting the world as never before
Conduct the symphony O, King!
    We implore You, let Your music thrill us
    Higher and higher
    Let us go
    Let us soar like never before
Cascading love bringing Heaven to earth
    Visitation songs we imitate here on earth
    From Your throne…bringing nations new birth
Your people cry out, You hear and respond
    Let me in
    Make room for me
    I am key at this time
The harvest, Your harvest, Your people, they come
    Your watchful eye is upon us
    Surely as the sun sets, there is much more
    Your people, You come!

The Kingdom Maker

Lord, I am a partaker of Your divine nature first of all
That's my pearl!
You have allowed me to see into Your heart and into
    my heart—that is my part
That releases unseen and unheard of things important
    to You—for the world to see and experience
You cloned us, each one who is open for more of You
As You transform us into Your likeness, we are on our
    way to adventure and supernatural capabilities
You have the canvas in front of You
Liberty and design plans are a breeze
You are at ease
Constant creation is swirling in You
You twinkle and make turns with glee—who could
    imagine this could be me!
Really, Lord, You have more in store for me?
How could that possibly be?
You want to amaze me
You want me to experience more and more of You
You want me ready for more and more of Heaven here
    on earth, don't you?
The supernatural is the natural I want also
Let it pour
I want more!

Endless Rhymes

The endless supply—it is there, have no care
I pick up where I left off yesterday
There is more today and I don't pay a red cent for it!
Has anybody's thoughts been just like mine—no—my
    writing, similar perhaps, but not exactly!
How keen to be seen in such light and what flight and
    altitude I gain when I'm on that plane
No entrance fee to pay—no admission
I have an everyday pass!
It is such fun to run and jump and be myself and be
    free!
I have a key!
My key is big and noticeable and light weight!
Thank You, Dearest One, for everything You give to
    me
I am most appreciative
You are so readily available
I am in awe of wonderful You
Thank You, thank You Most High God and Sovereign
    King
My cup runs over—spilling over the brim
Niagara Falls, You call, I answer
Our communication is wonderful
Where can I go from Your Spirit, You are there!
You are everywhere!

Psalm 139

It is so good to be in Your presence

Like breathing high octane air—filtered perfectly!

Life giving for sure

There is no end to the rhymes

A composition in verse that rhymes

Correspondence in terminal sounds (as of two lines of
verse)

Rhythm—regular rise and fall in the flow of sound in
speech

Rhyme and rhythm are together in the dictionary

When writing poetry, I can feel and hear the rhythm
like a beat

Rhyme

Rhythm beauty in these words

Chapter Eight

Invitation

One Sunday afternoon, a delightful surprise awaited my husband and me as we boarded a Malaysia Airline flight on the Island of Penang. We had been outstation, as they say, for the weekend ministering at a church there. Our short destination flight would take us to Kuala Lumpur, the capital city of Malaysia.

The flight originating from London was crowded as we boarded the plane. We found our assigned seats. As I began to focus on the woman I would sit beside, I heard the Lord speak to my heart and say, "I want you to prophesy to her." I was willing. Engaging in conversation with her was easy. 'Lord, this is fun,' I thought. My grandparents were born in Ireland as she had been, and our plan was to return to minister there again. I asked questions and mentioned we were ministers hoping it would open a door. We shared and connected. Her mother had recently died and she was going to visit her aunt in Australia. I prophesied and told her, "When you get to Australia, you're going to meet people, even relatives that can help you. God is going to help you get a job when you go back home." The conversation flowed as the clock ticked away on this brief but amazing ride.

As the plane started approaching the Kuala Lumpur Airport, my posture suddenly changed. I sat very close to her and began to share God's plan for her life, boldly emphasizing that I was not talking about religion. I was telling her about Jesus who wanted to have a personal relationship with her. My husband immediately started to pray. She listened intently as I told her how much God loved her. The light was green. I proceeded asking her if she would like me to pray with her. Having our sins forgiven and receiving Jesus as our personal Lord and Savior is what we must do to receive the gift of eternal life in order to go to Heaven.

"Would you be willing?" I asked.

She said, "Yes!"

We prayed together as the plane descended. Touching down on the tarmac, after 39 minutes of airtime, the assignment was complete. Imagine my thrill to hear her words, "I feel much better." My grateful heart danced and the angels in Heaven rejoiced! It's so encouraging to witness people getting saved.

Jesus had just introduced Himself to a precious soul in need of a magnificent Savior. This was His divine encounter He loves to have with people. Anytime, anywhere, all over the world. If you would like to give your life to Jesus or recommit yourself to the Lord, pray this prayer:

Father, forgive me for any sin I may have committed, both knowingly and unknowingly. Thank You for dying in my place and washing me clean. Thank You for Your love for me. I accept Your Son, Jesus, as my Lord and Savior. Because of this belief and because of this confession, if this is my first time praying this, I am now a Christian. If I was far from You, I am reconnected to You. Today is the beginning of the rest of my life. Great days are here for me. In Jesus' Name, Amen.

Jesus said, *"Most assuredly, I say to you, unless one is born again, he cannot see the kingdom of God"* (John 3:3). If you prayed that simple prayer, you were just born again and have gained access to the Kingdom.

Once people give their life to the Lord, they often don't know what the Lord gives to them. Not knowing what the Lord gives to us may cause us to think salvation is the end when it's actually the beginning. The day we gave our life to the Lord, it was the end of who we were and the beginning of who we are becoming. Celebrate the progress we've made in our journey as born again Christians. Take what we've learned and share it with others so they too can wear God's presence.

We were handpicked by God, but do we realize what we have in Him? So much hope and direction. All we have and have in Him—through Him, at all times. We have escaped the world's darkness and have gained insight from His perspective. We hold it and have been truly blessed. We are in a very special place because we need to be. The Lord has blessed us so we may be a blessing—His honor, His help and gratitude, and just blessings galore. We stand strong, full of honor and care for people. We carry His presence well. He will use us in an honoring position. Be open and ready for what God has called us to do. He's been good. He's been faithful. He's been consistent. He made ways when there was no way. He's a good Father. Clap your hands and rejoice in the Lord. Give Him all the glory, honor and praise.

The Father Heart of God

You are created with God's plans and purposed in mind

You are not a burden to Him

He cares for you like no other can, as only God desires

He designed you perfectly with His intentions to fulfill you and satisfy His goals

He is the only "perfect Father"

He dreams big dreams for you that will thrill your heart and delight His

He cheers you on so you can be successful

He cheers you on so you glorify Him

He made you in His image and likeness

You are not a mistake to Him

To God be the glory for the things He has done

Dare to Dream Big

Look and see the transparency
Personal revival is in store
No hidden agenda, clarity for sure
Get hold of the real stuff, we are not poor
Enjoy your share, it is right there
Ask and you can have it
Like manna, like the loaves and fishes multiplied
Dare to dream big, I implore, you get to the core
So you can be poured out

ABOUT THE AUTHOR

Patricia Anne Rooney (also known as Pam) follows God according to the prophetic word He speaks to her. Without fail—it is irresistible. God gave these words to Patricia on Christmas morning when she started to write this book: "I want to use you to captivate hearts."

She believes wholeheartedly the invitation is available and will open the wells and lead people in the right and new direction He has for them. Fullness of joy for everyone who believes and receives.

Patricia has ministered in five continents including the countries of Venezuela, Australia and Southeast Asia. She has also ministered and taught at YWAM bases in Australia and the United States, as well as ministering at Women's Aglow and other women's events and conferences.

In 2001, the Lord told Patricia she was an outspoken vessel for Him. Paint brush in one hand designing, a pen in the other hand to write, and a voice to proclaim. He was ready to bring that talent into the light where the Holy Spirit could infuse it. It was her creative calling to write this book.

God used Patricia to be a mouthpiece of comfort and direction for the Kingdom and His people. He used her to set things in order. She sees things with His eyes. When changes need to be made, the Lord can count on her to smooth things out His way, without delay, so they do not decay and are not ruined completely. He has given her keen insight and a perfect way to deliver it.

While composing this book, there was quite a battle going on, but things turned around in Patricia's favor, allowing her to see the light at the end of the tunnel. Praise God! She was able to complete that which was started and now, she is celebrating the victory.

A Letter to God

Dear One,

You have invited me to be a messenger to Your people early on in my walk with You. What a glorious experience it has been. Thank You for bringing me close to You and teaching me and allowing me to have a never ending love for Your people and Your Word. I want to share this amazement so people will benefit greatly like I did.

What about the book You have given me to write?

Patricia A. Rooney

God's Rich and Fulfilling Response

Patricia,

I have positioned you powerfully in the middle of this book's influence. This book is a vehicle I use to announce and declare My excellence and display Myself—using one person's testimony…yours.

You paint a picture for people, for My people, to know how to draw closer to Me with their own style. It will be contagious and successful, bringing the "new" as well as surprises to My people.

Your Heavenly Father